Vintage

VALENTINES

Coloring Book for Kids

Volume 1

Emilia Potter Prince

Blue Goose Press

DEDICATION

This fun coloring book is for my wonderful Valentines–
Ben, Ella, Karsten, Joey, Hayden, Libby, Dibby and little Coming Attraction Baby Girl
and for all the children in the world who love Valentine's Day.

If I were a Rose
in the Garden,
All trembling, wet with the dew,
I'd lift my eyes to my Valentine
And tell him I was true.

HELEN E. JEFFERS.

To my Valentine.

At thy dainty little feet
I lay my homage low,
Deign with a loving thought to meet
One who for thee doth glow.

MY VALENTINE
WHETHER VALENTINE'S DAY IS ROSY
OR BLUE
DEPENDS ENTIRELY, MY DEAR, ON YOU

*Let me
be your Valentine.*

I want to send a valentine
A pretty one to you
But it takes a lot of courage
Such a bold, bold thing to do.

For my Valentine

I'm ready,—
if your love
is true,—

To offer now My Heart to you.

Smiles
And kisses most are needed in
the winter time. That's the
reason I have pleaded
Be my Valentine.

For my
True Love

Oh, Daisy dear
I love you,
will you be
my Valentine?

I long
to hear you

promise
that you'll
be for ever
mine.

To My Sweetheart

MARY- ELEANOR- GEORGE-

Telling the Secret.

For my
Sweetheart

In festoons of roses
your heart I'll
entwine

If you will but
love me my
sweet Valentine.

As long as you're
MY VALENTINE,
In love's sweet prison I won't pine.

VALENTINE GREETINGS

Either rain or shine
Or any other weather
Would suit me fine,
If we could be together.

VALENTINE GREETING

Mercy me! Am I in love?
Do tell me what's the matter!
Every time I look at you,
My heart goes pitter-patter.

ABOUT THE AUTHOR

Emilia Potter Prince was working on her biology degree when a summer job sent her in a completely new direction. Counseling at a summer camp made her realize that she absolutely *must* work with children and art. She has stayed on that path ever since, producing delightful books and art for children. "I have found my true passion," Emilia says, "and children are at the center of it."

Emilia delights in seeing people explore and enjoy art. Vintage Valentines Coloring Book for Kids is the first volume in her new series of unique and charming coloring books for all ages, scheduled to appear periodically throughout 2014 and beyond.

Made in the USA
San Bernardino, CA
05 April 2014